"Let go of
your mind
& then be
mindful."

RUMI

The life of a man is a circle from childhood to childhood, and so it is in everything where pow- er moves. Even the seasons form a great circle in their changing, and always come back again to where they were. The sun comes forth and goes down again in a circle. The moon does the same, and both come back the same, and both are round. Birds make their nests in circles, for theirs is the same religion as ours. The wind, in its greatest power, whirls. The sky is round, and I have heard that the earth is round like a ball, and so are all... Everything the Power of the World does is done in a

"

BLACK ELK

A Mindfulness
Coloring Book

COLOR
yourself
CALM

Written & compiled by
Tiddy Rowan

Mandalas by
Paul Heussenstamm

BARRON'S

Introduction

Mindfulness

Peace of the Soul

Day After Night

Dance of the Butterfly

Light of Heaven

Moon Goddess

Copper Circle

Pathfinder

Fruit of the Soul

Ocean Rainbow

Indian Colors

Tibetan Sun

Chartres Hologram

Sun within the Sea

Nature's Kitchen

Black Crown

Ancient Future

Force Behind the Wolf

Sri Yantra

Red Snake Dream

Lotus with Eyes

Eternal Living Flame

Indian Flower

Firing Love Bloom

Feather Mandala

Rainbow Ananda

Black African Flower

Man in a Maze

Full Rainbow of Being

Out of Hands

Chakra Wheel

Electric Hearts

Happiness of the Soul

Inner Peace

About the
quotes

About the
illustrator & author

INTRODUCTION

Color Yourself Calm is a mindfulness-inspired coloring book including 33 original color mandalas with their accompanying black-and-white templates to color in. Inspirational quotes and mindfulness techniques accompany each image to enhance the experience. Mandalas are designs that draw your eye toward their centers, and in doing so, focus the mind. Coloring in mandalas relaxes the mind, body, and spirit, relieves stress, and is a chance to explore your own inner creativity.

Historically, mandalas are ancient forms of meditative art: the symmetrical, concentric circles are designed to ease the overloaded mind and release its deep-rooted creative and expressive inclination. By becoming absorbed in coloring in an object of beauty, the reader will embark on a practical exercise in mindfulness. This is an easy way to relax the mind, body, and spirit, while subconsciously developing self-knowledge, expanding the imagination, and creating a sense of well-being.

The first mandalas were almost certainly created as far back as the fourth century by Buddhist monks as an art form on which to meditate. Mandalas are found in deeply rooted and diverse cultures and religions across the world, wherever there is an impulse to tap into an unexplored part of the mind or spirit.

Psychologists (pioneered by Carl Jung) have observed that people with no grounding in Eastern mysticism draw mandala-like shapes spontaneously in psychotherapy. Such drawings are thought to represent an attempt by the conscious self to recognize and integrate unconscious knowledge. A mandala, in this light, reflects the inner expression of the person creating it—tapping into the subconscious and connecting to a deeper part of the psyche or soul that is not easily expressed in the language of words. So, relax, unwind, and explore your inner subconscious by coloring yourself calm!

Kurukulla Mandala
TIBET, NINETEENTH CENTURY

MINDFULNESS:

PRACTICE

Practicing a simple mindfulness exercise before getting started helps to center your attention. Sit in a comfortable but upright position, drop your shoulders, and follow each breath for a few moments. Turn your attention to whichever mandala attracts you the most. Let your conscious mind follow the imagery, circles, and cycles until you reach the center of the mandala. Become aware of the colors and immerse yourself in the imagery.

The objective is to empty your chattering mind and focus on the images in the mandala. If your attention wanders—focus once again on your breathing and return to the image. Use the center of the mandala as your anchor to return to when you feel your concentration wandering.

Gradually, shift your focus to the mandala template on the right-hand side of the page and start to color it in. You can follow the colors in the picture or you can choose your own colors at random, selecting those that appeal to you for any given section.

As you color in, keep your attention on the activity, parking your mind into neutral so you can access your subconscious. Areas of your deeper self are then able to come to the surface and communicate with your conscious mind.

This also gives your right brain (emotional, instinctive, and imaginative) a chance to interact with your left brain (logic and reasoning) so they can disentangle problems and recreate a sense of balance. See it as a way of letting your instincts become apparent.

There is no right or wrong way to access the mandalas. Just the action of looking and staying within their framework is an exercise in practical mindfulness. These guidelines are simply to help you find your own individual response.

The three key ingredients to being mindful are time, patience, and attentiveness. So stop, sit, be still, and look mindfully into a mandala, begin coloring, and let your inner adventure begin ...

EXERCISE

The essence of the discipline is in the word mindfulness—
being mindful—and not "mind full." Use your breathing as an
anchor and access point to the state of being mindful and it will
strengthen your mind by keeping it focused.

It's easy to read a few words on the importance of your
breathing or the value of being mindful of what you say to
others, not dwelling on things you cannot change or future
events that may not happen. But practicing it, actually
connecting to mindfulness, takes commitment to begin. All the
benefits will become apparent as soon as you decide to engage
with it. And like everything—it gets better with practice.
Eventually, it will empower and encourage you to take more
and more steps, until you become mindful in all the activities
in your life. The mandalas in this book will reinforce the
importance of staying in (or returning to) the here and now.
Selecting a mandala to color in and keeping your mind focused
on a single thought—or simply the activity itself—is an exercise
in mindfulness. As you develop this practice, it becomes easier
to apply mindfulness in other areas, to pay more attention to
everyday activities and to focus on your breathing whenever you
need to reach for a moment of calm.

BREATHING

A deeply relaxed person breathes around seven times a minute.
Slow your breathing down and you will automatically relax.
This is helpful when you need to focus before an important
interview or presentation, during periods of stress, or simply to
keep calm.

Breathe in (count to five—approximately)

Hold it (count to two)

Breathe out slowly (count to five—approximately)

Repeat, a couple of times then allow your breathing to find its own
slower rhythm without forcing it.

Peace of the Soul

Be mindful—not mind full.

Day After Night

Live in the present moment.
Only be aware of what is happening right now.

Light of Heaven

"My religion is very simple. My religion is kindness."
DALAI LAMA

Moon Goddess

The center doesn't have to be "out there."
It can be the center of your mind or your self.

Copper Circle

By concentrating on coloring in, worries of
the past and anxieties about the future dissipate.

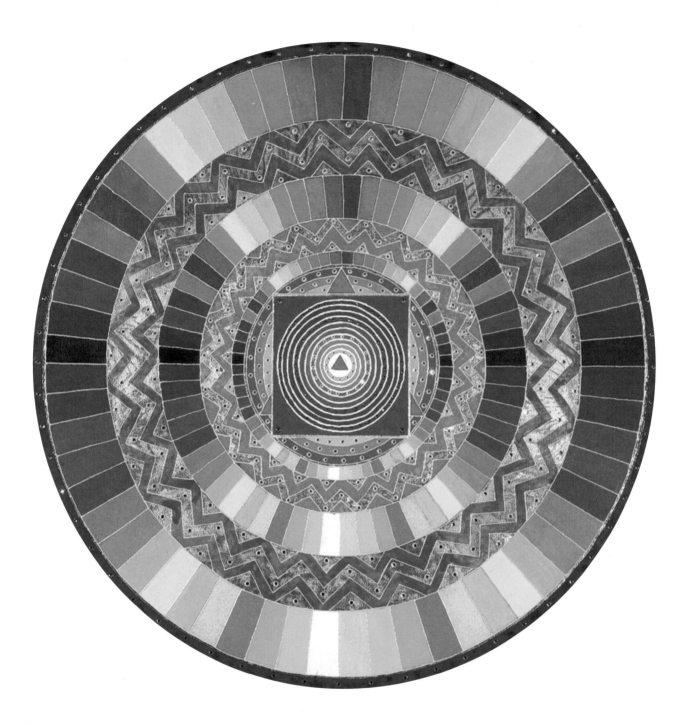

Pathfinder

"A person who never made a mistake never tried anything new."
ALBERT EINSTEIN

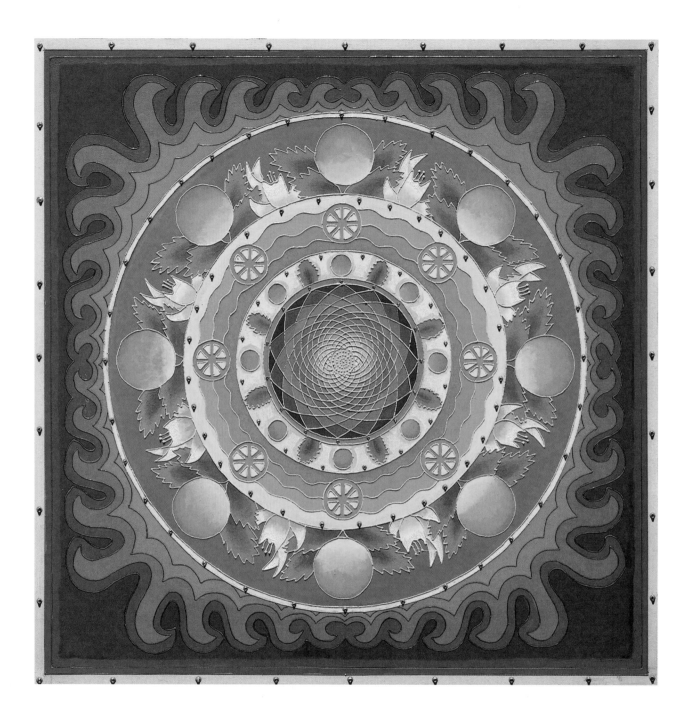

Fruit of the Soul

*"Happiness resides not in possessions, and not in gold,
happiness dwells in the soul."*
DEMOCRITUS

Ocean Rainbow

The spectrum of colors reflects positive energy.

Indian Colors

Be mindful of feeling centered.

Tibetan Sun

*"The secret of health for both mind and body is...
to live in the present moment wisely and earnestly."*
BUDDHA

Chartres Hologram

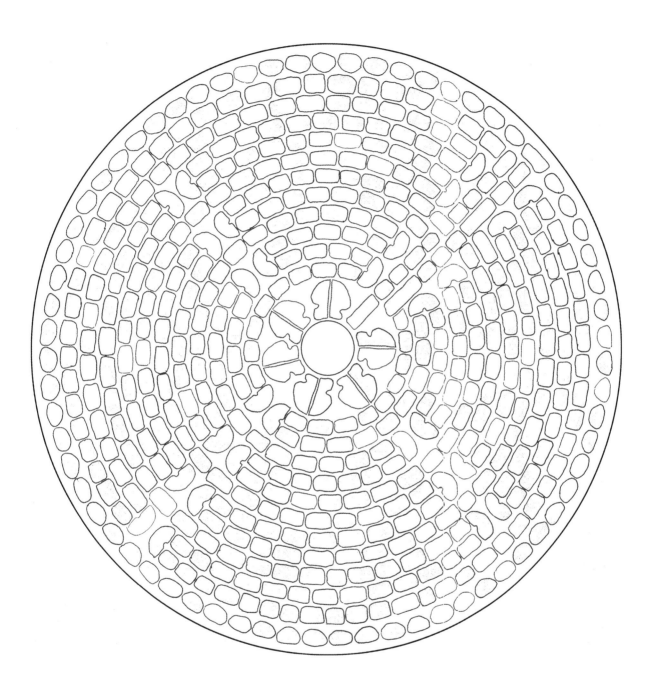

View the world with a positive outlook and
the reflections cast upon you will be beautiful.

Sun within the Sea

*"Chance is always powerful. Let your hook be always cast;
in the pool where you least expect it, there will be a fish."*
OVID

Nature's Kitchen

Let the natural healing process revive
and restore your mind and body.

Black Crown

Focus on the inner dot. Allow your mind's eye to create different patterns and illusions, which will center you and give you a feeling of calm.

Ancient Future

*"What lies behind us and what lies before us are
tiny matters compared to what lies within us."*
RALPH WALDO EMERSON

Force Behind the Wolf

Let your imagination roam free.

Sri Yantra

Be mindful of the powerful energy within you.

Red Snake Dream

"Sometimes dreams are wiser than waking."
BLACK ELK

Lotus with Eyes

There are more ways of seeing than just looking straight ahead.

Eternal Living Flame

Be mindful, as you color, of drawing energy in from the sun.

Indian Flower

Focus on a particular problem. Gradually, untie those
knots as you color towards the center of this mandala.

Firing Love Bloom

"*I found I could say things with color and shapes that I couldn't say any other way—things I had no words for.*"
GEORGIA O'KEEFFE

Feather Mandala

"Let your life lightly dance on the edges of time like dew on the tip of a leaf."
RABINDRANATH TAGORE

Rainbow Ananda

Spend a few moments soaking up the gentle
feeling of this calming mandala.

Black African Flower

Face your fears and overcome them through
the process of coloring them out.

Man in a Maze

Let your right brain and left brain meet and work together in the center.

Full Rainbow of Being

The mind is a workshop full of busy ideas, thoughts and worries.
But deep in the center there is a stillness, where the inner self
is protected from the mind machine. Find this center through
coloring yourself calm.

Out of Hands

"What is a friend? A single soul dwelling in two bodies."
ARISTOTLE

Chakra Wheel

**Be mindful of the enormity of the cosmos
and our place and purpose within it.**

Electric Hearts

"Love is the only reality and it is not a mere sentiment.
It is the ultimate truth that lies at the heart of creation."
RABINDRANATH TAGORE

Happiness of the Soul

Color in your happiness.

Inner Peace

"It isn't enough to talk about peace. One must believe in it.
And it isn't enough to believe in it. One must work at it."
ELEANOR ROOSEVELT

66 A mandala is a very ancient guide that symbolically allows you to visually look into yourself. The process of coloring in a mandala can give you profound insights into your psyche and your mind. It appears simple, and it is, yet there are layers of growth and understanding and even a transforming of consciousness that are revealed in a mandala painting, whether coloring one in or simply looking at one. The truth about mandala meditating is just to sit still and gaze upon one. Once you have colored in several mandalas – or even several parts of one mandala – you will begin to feel patterns within yourself. This is valuable because it allows you to recognize patterns and begin to communicate with your conscious self through these core patterns. 99

PAUL HEUSSENSTAMM

QUOTES ARE TAKEN FROM:

ALBERT EINSTEIN was a theoretical physicist. He is renowned for developing the general theory of relativity and received the Nobel Prize for Physics in 1921.

ARISTOTLE is one of the greatest philosophers from ancient Greece. His work has had a long-lasting influence on the development of all Western philosophical theories.

BLACK ELK was a famous holy man, traditional healer and visionary of the North American tribe of Oglala Lakota (Sioux).

BUDDHA is the founder and original teacher of Buddhism.

CARL JUNG was a revolutionary psychiatrist and psychotherapist. He is best known for having founded analytical psychology.

DALAI LAMA is a high lama, guru and teacher of Tibetan Buddhism.

DEMOCRITUS was known as the "laughing philosopher," who influenced modern science more than any other pre-Socratic philosopher.

ELEANOR ROOSEVELT was an American politician and the longest-serving First Lady of the United States.

GEORGIA O'KEEFFE was a twentieth-century American painter who focused on finding abstract forms in nature for seven decades.

OVID was a Roman poet whose work strongly influenced more recent European art and literature.

RABINDRANATH TAGORE was a Bengali poet, novelist, and painter. He won the Nobel Prize in Literature in 1913, the first non-European to do so.

RALPH WALDO EMERSON was an American preacher, philosopher, lecturer and poet, and the leader of the Transcendentalist movement.

RUMI was a thirteenth-century Persian poet, theologian, and Sufi mystic.